I Walk on the River at Dawn

Joanne Hart

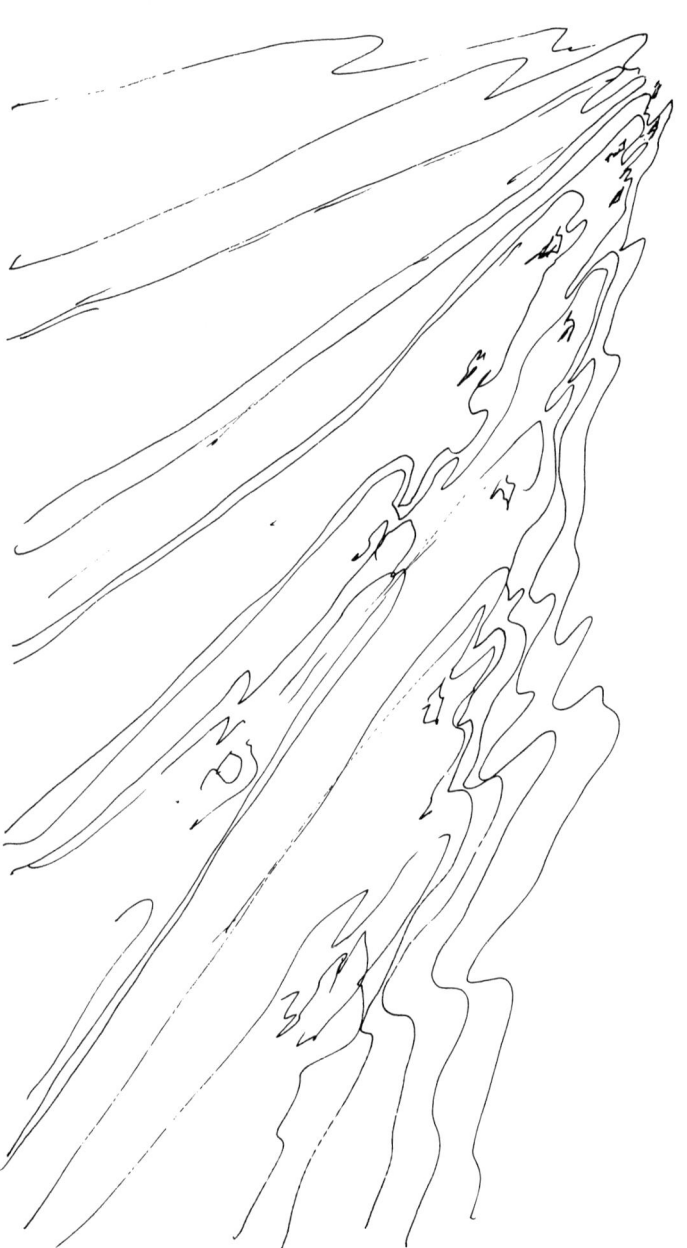

I Walk on the River at Dawn

Poems of Winter

Joanne Hart

Drawings by Betsy Bowen

Women's Times Publishing
Grand Marais, Minnesota

Some of these poems have first appeared in: *Great River Review; Sundog; Sing Heavenly Muse!; WARM Journal; Milkweed Chronicle; Zenith City Arts; Verbal Events; Women's Times.* Milkweed Editions included "I Walk on the River at Dawn" in the anthology *The Poet Dreaming in the Artist's House,* and also published "Spider Sun" as a broadside, woodcut by Betsy Bowen.

The collection is for Joseph
who was the last to leave
the children's cabin,

and for Nathaniel

I Walk on the River at Dawn. Copyright© 1986 Joanne Hart. Drawings © 1986 Betsy Bowen. Printed and bound in the United States of America. All rights reserved. No part of this book may be reproduced in any form or by any electronic or mechanical means including information storage and retrieval systems without permission in writing from the publisher, except for a reviewer, who may quote brief passages in a review. For information contact: Women's Times Publishing, P.O. Box 215, Grand Marais, MN 55604.

First printing 1986

ISBN 0-910259-05-4

CONTENTS

Daughters 5
Raven Winter 7
Country Sauna 9
Autumn 10
A Bear in the Apple Tree 11
Feel the Winter Coming On 13
Solstice 15
I Walk on the River at Dawn 16
The Moon Between Us 17
Dreamcatcher 19
Metamorphosis 20
"Art is Only a Tangent" 23
Running the Dogs 26
Icy Road 28
Widows in Late Winter 29
Lost Friends 31
Highway 61 32
Making it Down to Portage 33
Wilfred Montferrand 35
Spider Sun 37

DAUGHTERS

They rise Rhine maidens, straining young
bodies from the pulling glitter,
breasts swelling in the sun,
thighs under crystal. As though
the rain fed their bones
and streamed in them, they grow
changed in each bathe,
stroke against the current,
turn, float fearlessly
down-river toward the bend.
Ice water ache moves at last
up legs, loins.
Fingers whiten.
From the stream
their snow hands touch me
on the summer heated rocks,
the mint bed and wild orchids.

RAVEN WINTER

This winter is in the raven's eye
the way this place was focused in a pilot's lens
a June bright sky decades ago:
the river from the west, the road, lie white;
clocks on a black margin tell me
altitude, date, time. The pilot with the camera
has crashed long since in waiting
Lake Superior, or still bushwhacking the north,
he flies from Thunder Bay
rich moose-hunters, prospectors for gold,
old fishing sports.

Remember trails we went by touch, not picturing
a whole terrain for fear
we should turn back? We were green
explorers of our geography,
our bodies new found land. Now in raven winter,
— long, high looks
poised on cold air, a glide to breathe, to hear
echoes off rock, river ice —
winter away from you, I magnify the fates
that net our palms, old
photographs, maps from the air.

COUNTRY SAUNA

The women are made delicate by candlelight,
their nipples buds,
dark lichens patching their slender trunks.
They rest on sweet, clean smell of birch and heat.
The men are lean
with sinewed bark of young cedars.

Along benches they sit
bathing in their flowing sap,
thin branches still in still, hot air.

It is quiet, calm
ritual heritage of homesteaders
gone to the last purifying rite.

Now and again several leave,
stand on cold wet grass and talk.
Like the Arrow River, meanderer in these hills,
their glistening bodies mist in chill night air.
Pines darken the forest rim a meadow away.
Aurora pulses in the northern sky.

They return to heat, cold well water, rough brush,
but slowly, calmly
feeling together the sweet self pouring forth.

Later on the long drive
home through mountains
a lynx crosses ahead of them.

AUTUMN

Bones of the world are visible,
shapes of ridge and pass,
seductive curves of rock, hollows
where the run-off spins.
Clearly through the trees
we can see great beasts
rearing from compost of summer,
spruce fur spikey along flanks,
muscles flexed by mist and squally snow.
Now ermine and the snowshoe hare
are some time creatures, pied unknowns
imperfectly transformed. Pelts thicken.
Dusk creeps early out of tannic bogs
and dark holds to dawn. The deer
turn horned and greenish, rut.
Coupled to this naked season
we drop summer's disguise,
and before the camouflage of snow
masks identity, we stretch,
voluptuous rocky ridges,
feel the bones through the caress,
learn each from each the mutual
uncovering of mystery,
desire rising in the need to know.

A BEAR IN THE APPLE TREE

A bear is in the apple tree right by
the fire house, and just across the way,
perched on her stool behind the cash register,
Shirley peers out from the Trading Post.
Two days of the persistent scavenging.
"That old stinker," she says to me thinking
she could harvest apples though we both
know worms have reamed and reaped before the bear.
What holds us is what looks like bearish greed
but is the enviable thoughtlessness
that fills a craw and layers in the fat
before unbroken, dreamless winter sleep.
A small boy might have heaved and pulled himself
onto those crooked branches nothing like
the way this fearful sinew, pelt and claw
scuttled up the trunk as fast as thought.
The great black head with ears like exclamations
peers incongruously from the leaves
and makes us laugh in envy of the ease.

FEEL THE WINTER COMING ON

Drive back alone. The road's rebellious
with holes. Tree boles felled long ago, laid
to form a path across the chilly bog,
rise now from their asphalted graves
in humps and battered ends. The driving's slow.
Suddenly the way is barred by birds
whirling in the sleet. Their snowy wings
outspread like warning flags of coming cold,
snow buntings headed south swirl the arctic
weather in a net behind them. Stop
by the clearcut where the ragged sleeves
of mist change hills to lowering peaks, heavy
fists against the shuddering plantation.
Feel the winter coming on in clouds
of birds flight-bent by these declining days.

SOLSTICE

Name the world while the sun comes
later and later, chant against
bad news, hold the hem of light.
Watch how birds fill balsam near
the feeder. Lifts and landings wear
the branches smooth. Blue jays puffed
against cold wind give precedence
to bigger whiskey jacks. When
pine marten in its kingly fur
invades, takes away the suet,
no war cry sounds from chickadees.

Marten runs a beaten path,
overpasses through the thicket,
tunnels where drifts block the route.
A dozen birds watch as it scales
the tree and bears off chunks of fat.

Do what birds cannot: take
nails and hammer out to firm
the suet cage and weave coat-
hanger wire through the top.
Put food beneath a barricade.
Admit there are no simple acts,
since Eden only interventions.

Marten comes, primeval, shining
red and black, ears cocked. It sniffs
the boot marks, looks around, climbs
close to windows where the odds
are changed. Draw fierce, agile, stymied
beauty back and back, until
the sun tips balance in the sky.

I WALK ON THE RIVER AT DAWN

Wind has grained the snow,
left it the unplaned texture of old boards.
Feet sensitive, I feel
the path I cannot see
and shift aside the dust
blown deep in boot marks
on the water. Even cliffs
and trees are different now and give up
secrets unrevealed in summer. Far
from here, you cut with knives into a block
and ink it, phase on phase of changes
blacked to show a winter's texture,
to create by printing what the wind
proves here. In pale light
that shifts from north to east
I walk the river thinking of your print,
unlike, and yet as like as this will be
when I remember: how the cold
burned down the canyon, how I wept,
my face north into the blade of wind.

THE MOON BETWEEN US

Who would have thought the moon
could burn off mist, could step,
calm spider, outside her ring of augury
and sail into the clear?
Here a leading star above pines,
freshly made out of the fog,
shines in the stillness of the light.
Out on the path I listen for wolf, owl,
feel moon round on my cheek
tugging whiteness from snow,
drip from eave, hiss from coming rain.
If this white heat keeps up,
the river ice could go.
For you, too, moon is rising,
holding prairie with a layer of light,
painting the broad, flat sky.
Watch the east!
This thread, this silver line the moon spins,
paying out, retracting as she wanes,
dangles us, pale beads,
could slip us closer, or apart!

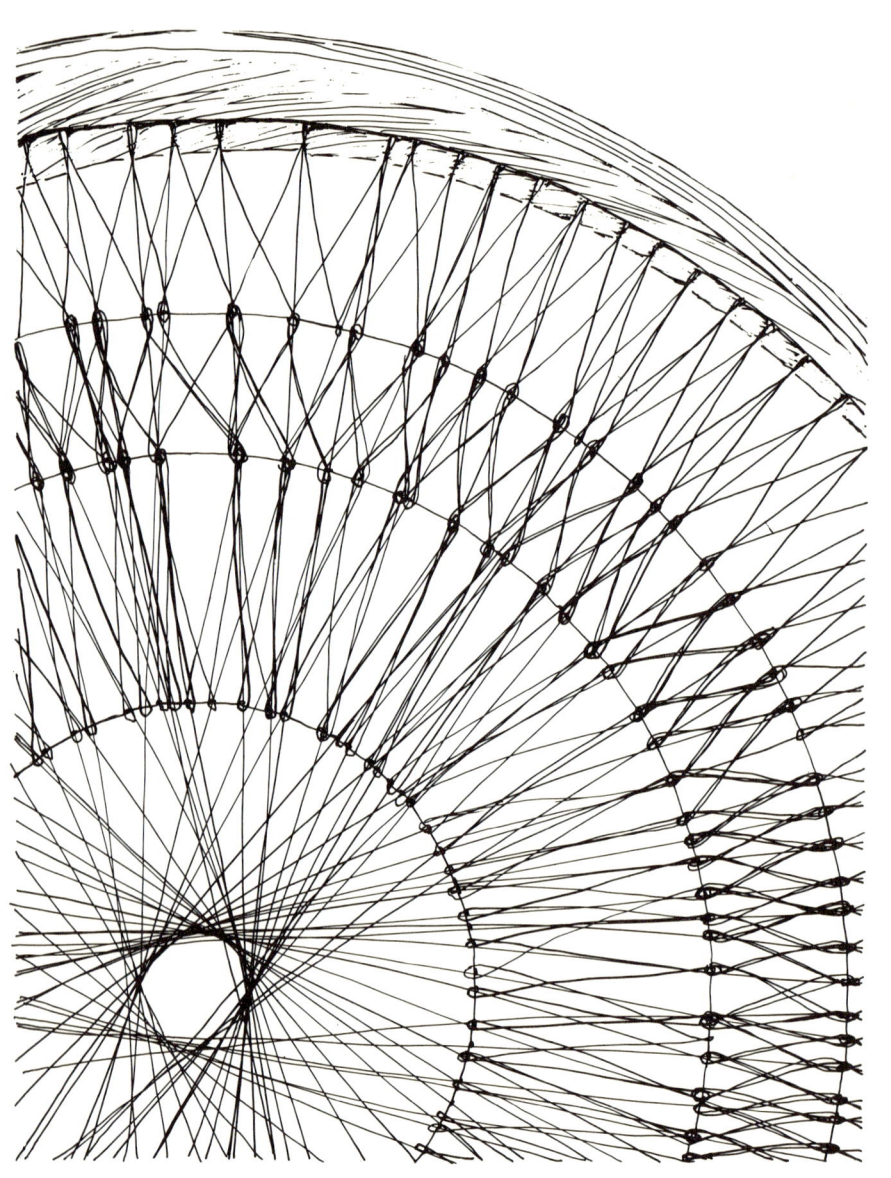

DREAMCATCHER

Scheme against dreaming: stay up late, set
the clock to ring before half-sleep can start
its morning journey.
                     No noise frightens me.
Scratchings by the window are the flying
squirrels come to feed on suet. Wind
rushing through ahead of weather change,
knocking branches, rattles pine cones down
the roof, worries the stove, showers the soot
into the chimney with sudden delicate whispers.
January-thawing eaves tap
drums of ice against the wall.
                            I keep
a flashlight by my bed, but that's old habit.
Waxing moon, aurora's glow reflect
light off a pure, white world. Better to lie
awake in this safe night and catch my breath
at glory stars. Better not to let
the sleep door open, or such darkness spills
that when I wake, I'm dream-dulled, not yet home.

METAMORPHOSIS

At the rare fine point of selfsight
comes a mask, the well remembered
hooded motherface with hostile eyes,
slipping over the reluctant consciousness
like cloth. In an instant glimpse
through those dead sockets
the glittering snowy spruce
turn grey, amorphous,
and the heart feels suddenly
another's beat, the dull constricted
drumming from the rocks below.

"ART IS ONLY A TANGENT"
— Beatrice Wood, sculptor

The wolf track from the lower meadow east
meets the trail of white-tailed deer and follows.
I can find no nervous step the deer makes.
Calmly she has crossed the road and leaped
the snowbank, calmly takes the lead to death.

Suddenly awake just after midnight,
Joseph hears coals drop, a fire sough
and settle in a giant stove, then three
long bursts of snarling, growling loud and close,
scary to a startled boy alone.

Daylight, I find her body near his cabin
door, and we begin translating signs
to story, what has happened here and how
we who create will tell it: blood and hair,
the body-shape inside a little thicket;

a dozen feet from here the doe lies, head
arched to her back, belly open, heart gone;
there's the wolf track, after the hunting miles
and kill, continuing up-river west;
no struggle. *When the moon laid out the grey*

and white world like a photograph, the doe
collapsed exhausted from her flight through drifts.
Or. *Snugly in the thicket, safely near*
our cabin door, the doe slept unaware
of stalking death. Falling coals, the snarls:

the body fiercely dragged, we speculate,
the tearing open of the kill. Wolf
steps its track next night to feed, moves on.
What's left is carcass where the warden spots
the half-healed bullet wound that slowed her range,

signaled to a wolf her role as prey.
Chickadees a few days peck at flesh.
There is a maze of marten prints. Some small
night creatures, maybe ermine, pygmy shrew,
run tunnels under February snow.

More snow. Nothing but a white mound. Sun,
reasserting power, makes the drift
a honeycomb with water drops that turn
glass beads at night. Dawn pulls toward equinox,
and I anticipate the corpse decay,

the stink, the final look of her, the grave.
But equinox brings blooming on the snow
mauve bouquets of ribs, the carcass gone,
signs drawing me again. I take up
the thread where wolves take up the thawing meat,

their tracks a web through trees to feeding sites.
Wolf hunger decimates the deer at last,
reduces her to spine, skull, teeth, hooves, scattered
cage, a winter's tale. Snow melts, and Bloodroot,
Single Beauty push up through the bones.

RUNNING THE DOGS

John walking stiff, cold
in his arthritic bones,
dances the yelping, bright, quick
sled dogs hindlegging down
along the traces, slips
their eager flexing into harness.
Rosanne in her golden hood
presses the sled bar to her ribs,
shouts to the dogs as she
cuts loose from the truck, and they
go like molten glass
over the snowy road.

They lean into the weight
and flow over the smooth road,
sinew, blood, bone
soundless save the pad
of twenty paws, the swish
of runners. Rosanne on her elegant
vestigial sleigh leaves
light lines and prints of dog
until next snowfall and the plow.
John follows her out
on wide, heavy treads.

In April, when the road is bare
and snow rots down through layers
of winter fall, in the woods
under tall storeys of pine
January's wolf prints
reappear embossed
and melt away like ghosts.

ICY ROAD

Like hurricane reports to Mahagonny
come weather warnings to this bell jar
island in the eye of winter:
dire road reports and constant ice.
Through melting pools at frozen culverts
we slide in a dream, roll
mornings in the dark fog of late winter, keep
alert for moose that loom and dare
us out of our momentum to the school bus.
I cannot stop to help you, tourist,
portager along the trail, tinkerer
beneath the raised hood of your car.
You eye my progress disbelieving me:
I come from nowhere like the moose with
calf, and I am disappeared into the fog and
gone on ice-and-dire roads
into the fastness of these woods.

WIDOWS IN LATE WINTER

It has been a winter of ice,
a widows' winter, keeping in
the griefs and rocking
desolations in the old recliner.
They have done a little beading,
but abstractedly and not for sale.
Come summer, and the cool wind
off the lake, they hope to work
and work away the loss.
In the Trading Post they drift alone
past pickled beets and soap,
picking up from shelves and setting back.
They fade but do not age:
their eyes are pale and innocent,
and growing always younger they will die,
the clear soprano still caught
in their wrinkled throats.
Between the eyes, fright
and shock have scored new grooves,
worn now as widow weeds.

LOST FRIENDS

We speak of them, friends
lost in Lake Superior. Bob rushed
headlong toward the rocky cove
and chased the boat adrift in wind,
frigid off-shore wind,
brittle clarity of stars.
Two brothers, daring river spate,
were swept miles out in frail
canoes and swamped. Friends disappeared,
David dropping weighted nets
that plunged the skiff below the fish,
others caught in storm and chop,
hands of heavy mist across their mouths,
tumbled, slowly rolling into crevices
of this great hungry lake,
the flashing beam from Isle Royale
a brief, white glitter down the swell.

Idle, lying in the sun
I dig my hands into the cobbled beach.
A boy plays near the water's edge.
You try the waves. Heavy
cliffs around us, pine trees,
breathe across the shallow bay.
Strangely compelled, I sort the smooth,
mysterious stones, earth bodies tumbled,
roiled and broken, worn,
worn away to sand.
Here the shadow outline of a face,
the eyes, a mouth that screams:
water-worn deposit in this bone-white
stone, this bird's egg piece of shore.
I close my hand now over songs not sung,
leaf and growth and seed
that will not come for friends.

HIGHWAY 61

This is a ghost trip. No one talks.
The faceless pair from Thunder Bay
sit apart. His boots are new.
She reads romance in paperback.
He waits for deer to cross the road.
The bus groans into morning past

birch and popple, pale sticks of old
forest. No trunk mighty, nothing
casts a shadow west. The road
unfitted to the flow of land
cuts by prehistoric shoals.
How the land resists the road!

It heaves, buckles, shrugs, rises
from the grave of ice and salt,
tar layers, stripe paint, hollow
bones of culverts, gravel beds.
Wind skirls a little snowy dust.
The busman lifts one finger from

his steering wheel: the spectral sign
each trucker gives him back before
they pass in phosphorescent veils.
Off-shore over the warm water
bitter cold raises Ghost
Dancers on an old, wild lake.

MAKING IT DOWN TO PORTAGE

Hochie, Allan, Jim and Steve
hang in the jeep off the Mt. Maud curve
and laugh. What a place
to get a flat, and the spare's as leaked
as a bleeding corpse.
Loggers waltz the icy hill and dance
the danger dance right by.
Popple bodies, sawed in lengths like trusting
girls in a stage-trick trunk,
go by stacked on the hauling rig trailing
diesel and death songs.
Hochie pumps and pumps the spare on Mt. Maud's
breast, up and down,
hands on ribs to air drowned lungs.

She'll make it down to Portage.

And late blooming snow
blown from seed clouds east
clings to shaman Steve
with bright
magic.

WILFRED MONTFERRAND

Wilfred, when you were young between world wars
a bright spring morning, and the sun heating
your cheek drew up summer from undergrowth,
you leaned on a downstream rail and smelled again
the rotting-sweet renewal in the woods
along the stream. Ice was brown and water
flowed in thin brown sheets on winter's crust.
Early insects ranged the melting snow,
piled still deep where Starflower would bloom.
You heard the puzzling rumble of thunder
from a clear blue sky and turning, saw
the house of ice, a jagged shifting mass
come bearing down, leaped, saw the bridge go,
heard the roar of fate and felt the chill.

Years later, briefly in the nursing home,
stranded there, a great blue whale among
the dying fish, you turned and turned a branch
of scarlet berries, mountain ash I brought.
It is too soon, you said, *I am too young,*
meaning for wreaths or burial alive.
A few more seasons at your cabin came
and narrow escapes, the sorts of saving leaps
we make from year to year that make our lives
until the bridge of flesh is swept away.

This spring, gnarled old apple trees in white
again, the sunlight freckled with their bloom,
I'll think of you and Henry in the park,
a twelve-pack on the bench between you,
laughter waiting under bee-filled trees,
the jokes, teasing talk, and then your bow,
the formal chivalry of your goodbye.

SPIDER SUN

Old spider sun has taken up the mess
of milky snowbanks round my place,
hitched herself a little higher in my sky,
and started spinning streams, brooks,
freshets by the roadside spilling over,
young, smelt-netting creeks.
Right here by my elbow the main
cord of her web, the Pigeon, flies
and hums and rattles day and night,
shaking out the rock-bed rhythm, bumping
banks and moving on down, moving down.
Why, just last week I brushed sooty
winter web flags from my rafters,
out my door, off my window. Oh,
see that sun, watch her pour
the run-off down my path!
So, tonight, what's this sister spider,
black and stealthy, creeping on my floor?
Let her be. I hear there's luck
in spiders and the web-shine red
at five a.m. gets me up, and out, and caught
again in hopeful new-leaf spring.

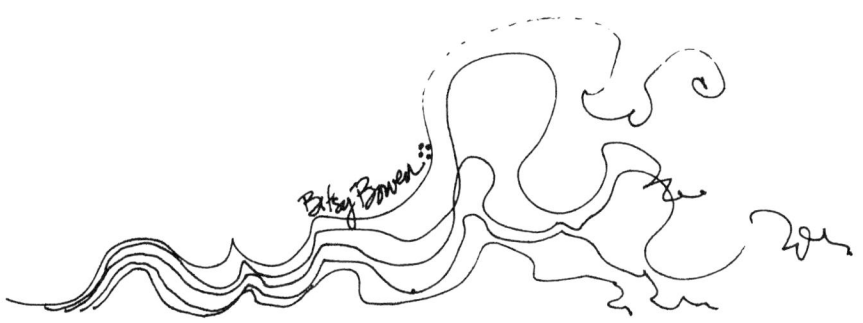

JOANNE HART, who was born in Weehawken, New Jersey, left the east coast to attend the College of St. Catherine in St. Paul. She has said that when she graduated in 1949 she turned into a Minnesotan. Now that her eight children have grown up, she lives alone during the months her husband is teaching away from home.

The family moved in 1974 to the ghost town of Pigeon River, an abandoned border crossing to Canada in northeastern Minnesota. Joanne Hart counts her years there in winters, and in this, her thirteenth winter, she has collected poems from what is the "fruiting season" for her writing. She is the author of two other chapbooks which reflect life on the Grand Portage Indian Reservation: *The Village Schoolmaster* (The Bieler Press, 1985) and *In These Hills* (Women's Times Publishing, 1982; second printing, 1986).

BETSY BOWEN works in pen & ink and woodcuts. For most of the last 20 years she has lived on an old homestead near the top of Good Harbor Hill, where she draws and does woodcuts of local subjects and northern scenes. She illustrated the *Women's Times Journal* for three years and has collaborated with Joanne Hart in the past, most notably in the 1983 Collaborating Artists "Mountains in Minnesota" broadside competition with the woodcut and poem "Spider Sun."